MARIJUANA: LET'S GROW A
POUND

A DAY-BY-DAY GUIDE
TO GROWING MORE THAN YOU CAN USE

by **SeeMoreBuds**

Marijuana: Let's Grow A Pound
A Day-By-Day Guide to Growing More Than You Can Use
Copyright © 2012 SeeMoreBuds

Published by Quick American
A Division of Quick Trading Co.
Oakland, CA

ISBN 978-1-936807-01-7

Executive Editor: Ed Rosenthal
Cover and Interior Design: Hera Lee
Photo Editor: Hera Lee
All Photos: SeeMoreBuds except for product photos on pages 5-7, 15, 18 and 138-140, which are property of R&M Supply.

Printed in China

INTRODUCTION

If you or your buddies smoked an eighth a day, every day, all year long, you would need an ounce of weed every eight days. This was the thought that started it all for me. I did the math: I was spending $60 a day for a sack that lasted me 24 hours. I figured that if I could grow a pound of weed in eight to nine weeks, I would have more than I could, would, or should smoke for more than four months.

My first attempt at growing 20 years ago was dismal. I was so eager to get started that I failed to do any homework. I've learned a great deal since then.

The intro that you are reading now is the longest section of this book. I have made it so that you can tackle the setup of the garden and its maintenance in short, simple steps. The set up is simple, yet one level more involved than shown in *Marijuana Buds for Less*, where only energy-efficient compact fluorescent bulbs were used in the garden.

Today, the would-be grower wants a pound of the finest herb using the easiest, fastest, most affordable method. In this book we follow two parallel grows, both using HPS (high pressure sodium) lights: Editor Ed Rosenthal challenged me to supplement the garden with CO_2 and compare the results. With the right equipment assembly I went ahead, laying the groundwork for you to follow along.

Hundreds of pounds have been grown and smoked by CEOs, pro athletes, and Fortune-500 executives, using the same methods you see in this book. And some of the weed you see in *Let's Grow A Pound* has actually been smoked by these high-level performers. They don't settle for second-rate weed, and neither should you.

Each time you do this grow it will be easier and more successful. By the third cycle, it will seem effortless. Take a deep breath and dig in. There is no easier method to growing a pound of the world's finest chronic.

~SeeMoreBuds

The first step is to select a location for your garden. Choose a safe, low traffic spot with convenient access to water, air and electricity. In this book you will see a closet location used for the garden. Each growing location is unique and will require some modifications, ingenuity, and imagination. Minimum space to grow a pound of chronic is 20 square feet, which is the size of our closet (2.6 x 8 feet). A 5 x 6-foot closet (30 sq. feet) would be ideal, providing greater access to the plants.

You will need to find your breaker box and make sure you have a free 15-amp breaker to run your 1000-watt garden. Only garden equipment should be plugged into outlets designated to the "garden" breaker. The 1000-watt HPS (High Pressure Sodium) bulb will use 9.5 amps, giving the garden another 5.5 amps for accessories (fan, etc.). All electrical items have a sticker on them that discloses the number of amps used by the product.

The first step is to gather materials to build the garden. Here is my list:

A.   C.A.P. 1000-watt Xtreme Digital ballast
B.   C.A.P. Xtreme LumenAire 6" air-cooled reflector
C.   C.A.P. 6" inline fan for carbon filter
D.   1000-watt HPS bulb (DigiLux brand pictured)
E.   Soil: three 64-quart bags of nutrient-supplemented mix for vegetables
F.   Carbon air filter that fits inline fan; here both fan and filter are 6" wide
G.   Lamp/appliance timer, with at least one "on/off" per 24 hours
H.   Thermometer
I.   Cloning tray
J.   Rockwool cubes
K.   pH tester and pH Up and pH Down

These supplies are not pictured but should also be collected:

- 18 3-gallon containers with drainage holes, and water trays to place the containers in
- Plastic tarp to line trays and protect floors from overflow
- Watering can
- Oscillating fan or centrifugal fan mounted to wall
- Panda white/black poly film, or other reflective material
- Ducting 6" wide to connect light reflector to fan
- Light mover (optional)

To supplement your garden with CO_2 you'll need this equipment (more details on pages 7 and 26):

- Second lamp/appliance timer
- 20-pound tank of CO_2
- CO_2 controller
- CO_2 regulator
- Drilled CO_2 tubing with micro holes (3-10 feet), and a plastic tubing T-connector
- Reflective foil or insulation to seal grow room

Recommended Lighting Equipment

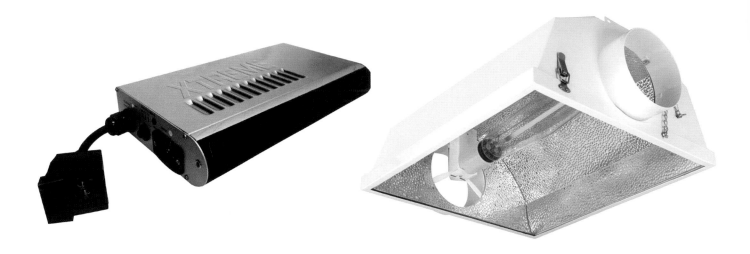

C.A.P. Xtreme Digital Ballast

Ballasts convert house current to the appropriate voltage for high intensity lights. Digital ballasts offer significant advantages over magnetic ballasts, as they are more power efficient, generate greater lumens, are lightweight, are silent, and emit less heat. The Xtreme digital ballast is a 1000-watt dimmable ballast with three separate power settings (50, 75, or 100 percent) for maximum lighting control.

C.A.P. LumenAire Air-Cooled Reflector

HPS and other high intensity bulbs emit intense heat that can build to lethal temperatures (for the plants) if left unattended. Air-cooled lights keep the garden from overheating by removing much of the heat before it reaches the grow room. Otherwise you need an air conditioner, which uses more electricity. The LumenAire reflector has 6-inch flanges for air cooling that attach to the air hose and inline fan. Its tempered hinged glass bottom allows for easy cleaning and bulb replacement.

Recommended CO_2 Equipment

PPM-4 Monitor

PPM-4 Meter

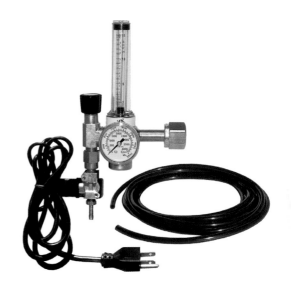

C.A.P. Fuzzy Logic™ PPM-2A CO_2 Controller

I opted for a top-of-the-line CO_2 controller. Like a good driver who gradually slows down before getting to a stop sign, the Fuzzy Logic controls the level of CO_2 without overshooting its target. It automatically dials in exact parameters for your area, learns how your garden uses CO_2, and adapts to keep levels constant.

C.A.P. PPM-4 CO_2 Monitor/Controller

When economy and simplicity are a priority, this is a great alternative. Mount the PPM-4 monitor to a wall, plug the PPM-4 meter into the power interface, then plug the CO_2 regulator into the PPM-4 meter. The LED monitor shows CO_2 levels at a glance—the indicator lights show the current level of CO_2 in your grow area.

C.A.P. REG-1 Regulator/Emitter

The regulator screws on to the CO_2 tank, and comes with an easy-adjust flow meter that allows you to preset your CO_2 flow level to meet room-size requirements. Each unit comes with 10 feet of undrilled micro tubing to disperse CO_2 throughout your room.

Cover the floor of the grow area with tarp and place water "catch trays" under the containers; this will reduce problems from overwatering, leaks, or unexpected water spills. The grow containers are arranged in rows three pots deep and six pots across. You can choose any configuration based on the number of plants you wish to grow.

It is important to pick quality strains. You are going to put real time, effort, and care into this grow. Choose a strain that you know will provide your desired results. The seeds used here are four well-known and easy-to-grow strains from TGA Seeds. You can also start with clones. The flags are made using permanent marker, duct tape, and toothpicks. They allow for quick and easy tracking of the strains. This is important, as you will see later.

Whether you are starting with seeds or clones, rockwool cubes provide an ideal moisture and oxygen-mixed medium, ideal for root growth. Before using the cubes, adjust their pH by soaking them in a large container with water, and add pH up or pH down until the water has a pH level of 5.0. Later, when plants are ready for soil, the water pH will be adjusted to 6.8 to 7.0. Being comfortable with pH adjustments is a cornerstone of successful gardening (more information on page 136).

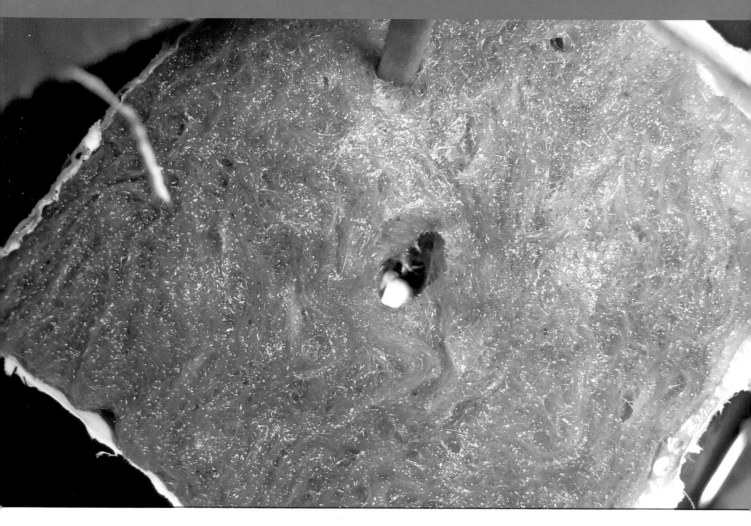

Allow the rockwool cubes to soak for a minimum of one hour. Once the cubes are adequately soaked, gently place one seed in the center of each cube. Push the seed about a quarter-inch below the surface.

Use the toothpick flags to label the strains. Later, you will be able to accurately clone your favorite strains. Keep the rockwool cubes in an area that stays between 70 to 85 °F and receives light at least 16 hours a day. A single 20-watt compact fluorescent light 8 to 12 inches from the cubes is ideal.

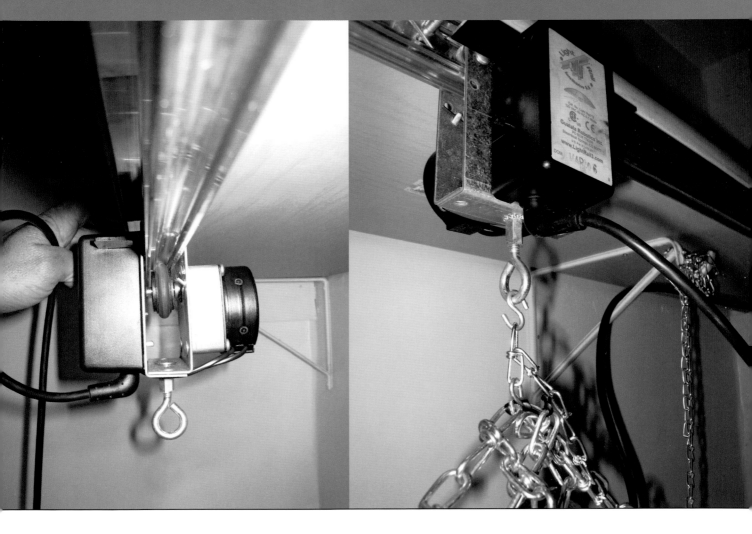

An optional light mover spreads light evenly around the room. A light mover slowly moves the light using a small electric motor which is attached to a steel rail. Most light movers can be installed in two positions, depending on which side you want the electrical cord. Here you can see the wheel running on the rail and the eyelet that the light hangs on. With this model you can adjust the distance the light travels.

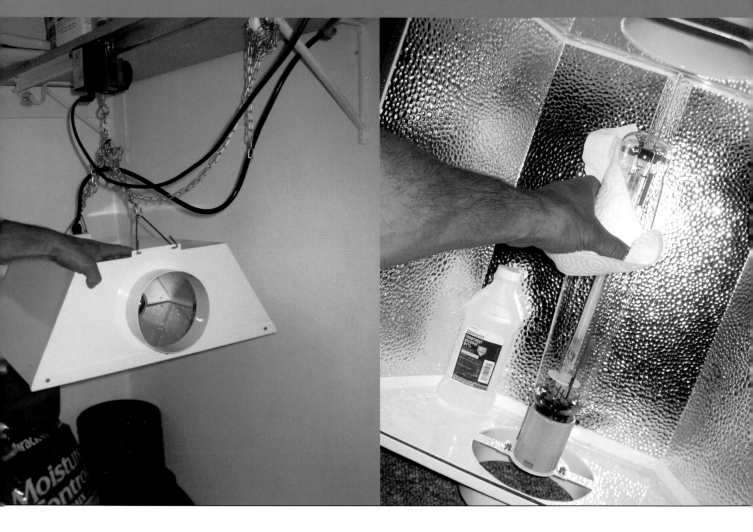

A shelf in the closet is tested to make sure it can hold the ballast and the light. The shelf is strenght-ened using ample support. Before turning on the HPS bulb, clean it with alcohol and a cloth to re-move all fingerprint smudges. A dirty bulb is in danger of getting "hot spots," reducing the bulb life.

The reinforced shelf is perfect for the ballast to sit on, out of danger of water spills. To tally the electrical usage running through the breaker, add the amps of each electric product. This should total no more than 80 percent of the load your breaker can handle: 80 percent of 15 amps = 12 amps. Some breakers can handle 20 amps. This concept also is applicable to extension cords and outlet multipliers. Make sure all extension cords and outlet multipliers are rated for 15-plus amps. Usually, 12- or 14-gauge cords are adequate.

To start, the hood can hang from the existing clothing rod or the unplugged light mover. There should be at least 3 feet between the ground and the bottom of the hood.

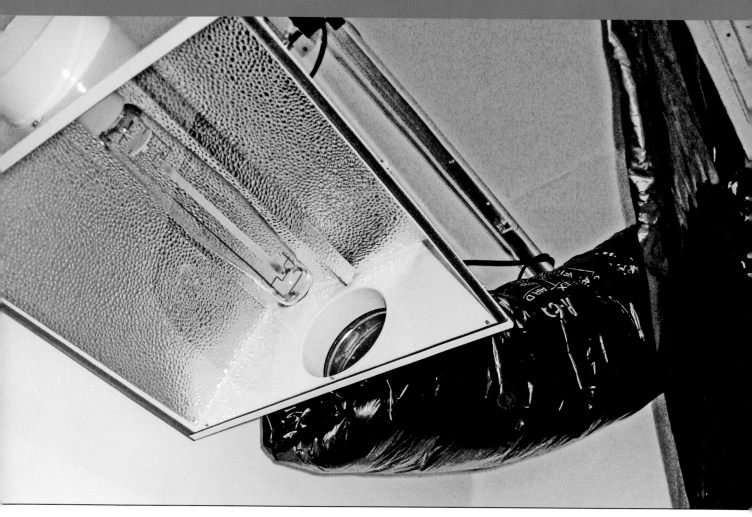

Attach the carbon filter to the light hood using insulated ducting. Pass the ducting through a piece of Panda film to stop light leakage. The purpose of the Panda film will become clearer as we move forward. Ducting can be purchased at any hardware store. Ideally, you will use insulated ducting to significantly reduce fan sound levels. Special foil tape should be used to attach ducting to the light and fan.

The insulated ducting passes through a hole in the Panda film, which is cut with pair of scissors. Tape the Panda film to the ducting to prevent light passing in or out of the grow room, white side in. Attach the inline fan to the ducting and place on the filter. The inline fan is placed so that the air is pulled from the grow room and blows into the carbon filter. The carbon filter will eliminate potent garden odors that could otherwise be detected blocks away.

Place seedlings under the HPS light, at least 36 to 48 inches from the light source, and covered with an object or material that will filter the light. The wicker domes shown are usually used to keep flies off food and work great to protect the plants. Alternatively, you can raise the light to about 50 to 60 inches above the plants, uncovered. Keep the medium moist, and watch seedlings closely for signs of stress during first the few hours under any new light source.

After two to 14 days all the seedlings should be visible (five to seven days is typical). The seedlings should be treated with care, and not touched or handled directly. The cubes should remain moist at all times. The cubes should **not** be soaked, completely saturated, or sitting directly in water. Remember: Roots need water and oxygen.

This garden is using 3-gallon containers. Both tall and short 3-gallon containers will be used to determine if one is better than the other.

Put a sheet newspaper at the bottom of containers to cover drainage holes. Fill the containers with soil, leaving 2 inches of space at the top. This garden is using Miracle-Gro soil, which has been premixed with nutrients by the manufacturer. After the first couple waterings, the soil will recede another 2 to 4 inches. Leaving this space at the top of the container provides space for watering and avoids messy overflows.

Gently remove the plastic from rockwool cubes before planting the seedling, and then bury the cube so that the top is flush with the soil.

If you use an organic or an un-supplemented soil, you will need to feed your soil with third-party nutrients. Start slowly and use moderation. It is easy to add nutrients as you go, and problematic to deal with nutrient overdose. Pay close attention to your plants and take careful notes. Balancing optimal levels of nutrients and optimal pH levels will secure you a large yield. Soil is a forgiving medium, which allows you a range of experimentation and correction.

After the seedlings have been placed in containers, put them under the light and water each container with a half-gallon of pH 7.0 water. Always use water with a pH of 6.8 to 7.0. The light should be no closer than 24 inches from the plants. Check on the plants frequently during the first 18-hour light period. If you are concerned that the light is too powerful and is injuring the seedlings, raise the height of the light. A gentle oscillating fan blowing between the light and plants will reduce stress on seedlings.

The CO$_2$ Factor

To increase yield, you can increase the number of lights, plants, and square footage of your garden. This will cost more in space, time, money, effort, and involve greater risk.

You can also increase your yield by adding CO_2 to your existing grow room, and watch your buds swell to the next level. Supplementing your garden with CO_2 is a bit more in cost and work but is by far the most efficient way to increase yield without buying more lights, plants, and space.

The CO_2 setup in this book includes the following equipment:
- 20 pound tank of CO_2
- C.A.P. Fuzzy Logic CO_2 controller (see page 7 for more info)
- CO_2 regulator (see page 7 for more info)
- Oscillating fan, or centrifugal fan mounted to wall
- Drilled CO_2 tubing with micro holes (3-10 feet), and a plastic tubing T-connector
- Lamp/appliance timer

Whenever you see this icon, you will find information pertinent to a grow supplemented by CO_2. We did a parallel grow with the CO_2 setup, and where relevant you will see notes on the CO_2 garden that tracks along with the day-to-day guide.

Place the CO_2 tank where it is easily accessed, as it will need to be refilled in about a month. It does not need to be in the closet. Attach the CO_2 regulator to the tank (screwed on). This is then attached to the CO_2 controller. Attach a length of CO_2 tubing to the tank's emitter (CO_2 regulator).

Make a loop with the drilled tubing with micro holes, and connect ends to the T-connector as shown above. Then attach the T-connector to the CO_2 tubing that runs from the regulator. Hang the loop 2 to 20 inches above the plants; it can be hung over the ducting or from the ceiling. The black tubing gradually emits CO_2 through its micro holes. As CO_2 is heavier than air, it will settle into the canopy of the garden.

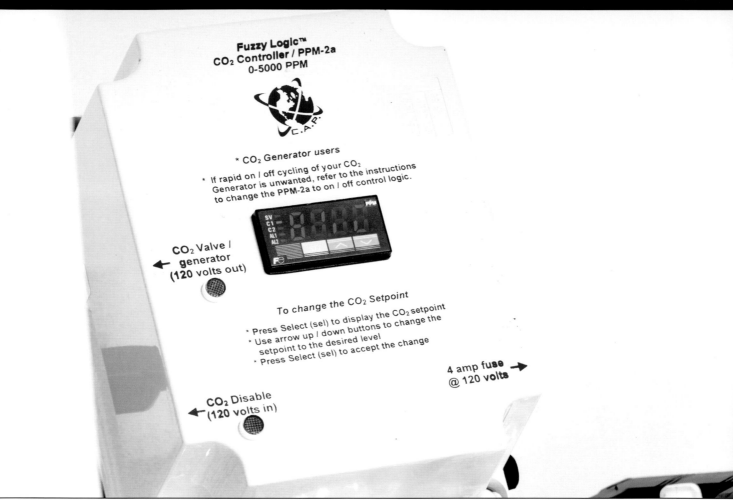

Plug the Fuzzy Logic Controller power cord into a timer, which should be set on the same time cycle as the lights. Plants utilize CO_2 only when the lights are on. The light timer and the timer for the CO_2 controller should always be on the same cycle. Use a fan set to "low" to disperse the CO_2 around the room. You want elevated CO_2 levels, 1000 to 1300 ppm, to increase yield and shorten harvest cycles!

The trickiest part of using CO$_2$ is maintaining a sealed room. Sealing your garden allows you to easily control CO$_2$ levels. However, you then face another problem: A sealed room has no place for heat to escape. A 1000-watt HPS bulb can cause temperatures to soar above 115 °F, killing your plants. One way to handle this excessive and fatal heat is to add an air conditioner unit, which offers superior temperature control. However, this consumes a lot of electricity.

We use another method: an air-cooled light. The light hood is sealed and exhausted using ducting and an inline fan. Ducting brings fresh air from outside into the grow room; this air passes through the sealed light hood and exits the room through another piece of ducting. The hot air created by the bulb is removed.

It is vital that the ducting and the light hood have an air-tight seal; any leaks in the exhaust sytem venting heat from the light could pull CO_2 from the room, depleting the CO_2 in several hours. Remember, the intention is to cool the bulb by bringing fresh air from outside the grow room, pass it over the bulb, and exit without mixing with the air in the grow room. This lessens the threat of overheating by removing the heat caused by the 1000-watt HPS bulb before it reaches the garden.

CO$_2$ can be introduced as soon as the seedlings appear. This book includes steps for both CO$_2$ and non-CO$_2$ growing. In either case, each garden will have its unique intricacies and quirks. Don't be intimidated: Once you take the first steps, stay patient, alert, and learn to make minor adjustments. Success is around the corner.

February 23, 2010—Assemblyman Tom Ammiano (D-SF) introduced AB390, The Marijuana Control, Regulation, and Education Act, a landmark bill to tax and regulate marijuana like alcohol and tobacco.

The seedlings directly under the powerful 1000-watt HPS light should be protected. Any object that filters light can be used.

"Change will
not come if we
wait for some
other person
or some other
time. We are the
ones we've been
waiting for. We
are the change
that we seek."
~Barack Obama

The light was lowered from 25 inches to 22 inches from the soil (this lowering should be done only if you are using a light mover). Soil was added to a few containers to offer support to seedlings that were leaning over or had collapsed under their own weight. The added soil is used to prop up the seedlings and give them support. Each plant received two cups of water. The room temperature has been kept at 74 to 79 °F.

Cannabis is indigenous to the Himalayan foothills.

The plants have green leaves, perky stems, and have grown overnight. They have serrated leaves which are the unmistakable trademark of cannabis. Some seed pods may still be attached to the foliage; leave them be. It may be more damaging to tear the seed off than to leave it attached.

"Every decision to control only breeds resistance, even the determination to be aware."
~J. Krishnamurti

The CO_2 tank is turned on today. The timer that controls the tank is set to the exact cycle as the timer for the lights. When the lights go on, the CO_2 injection in the room will start to be regulated and maintained at a level of 1200 ppm. Whenever you change the light cycle, the timer controlling the CO_2 also needs to be adjusted correspondingly. Plants use CO_2 only when lights are on.

America's first marijuana law was enacted at Jamestown Colony, Virginia in 1619. It was a law ordering all farmers to grow hemp.

There is an obvious difference in these two seedlings. The indica dominant strain (left) has thicker, darker green leaves. The sativa dominant strain (right) has slightly longer leaves. The second set of leaves is apparent in both. Soil was added to the containers that still had leaning plants. The light cycle was extended to 19 hours on, 5 hours off. Some leaves are a very light green. This is not a serious concern, but if it persists this could be signs of a nitrogen or pH problem.

A "presupposition" is an implicit assumption about the world or background belief relating to an utterance whose truth is taken for granted in discourse.

Four of the plants have grown three nodes (third set of leaves). All of the containers are rotated 180 degrees today. Rotating the plants is not mandatory but is recommended, to help with even light distribution.

Oaksterdam University was founded in 2007 by Richard Lee, who placed a provocative newspaper ad that proclaimed, "Cannabis Industry Now Hiring." Lee wanted to open a trade school for cannabis since visiting Cannabis College in Amsterdam.

Each plant is given 6 ounces of pH 6.8 water. The circled area is a node—the point on a stem where the leaf or branch is attached. The plants have established roots now and will grow a new node almost every day. Runoff water is tested, and has a pH of 6.5. This is good. Testing runoff water is a good way to measure the pH of the root environment. The more data you collect during a grow, the greater the resources you have for troubleshooting issues and for duplicating success.

"The greatness of a nation and its moral progress can be judged by the way its animals are treated."
—Mahatma Gandhi

The plants were pulled out of the closet today, rotated, and the light was lowered 2 inches (20 inches above the tallest foliage). When moving plants, pay extra attention for signs of potential problems such as water on the ground, pests, or mold. White reflective paper was added to the inside of the sliding closet door. Adding Panda film, white polyethylene, or other reflective material to the interior garden walls redirects light to the garden, making it visibly brighter.

CO₂

In 2009, pot was California's biggest cash crop, with annual sales reaching $14 billion. Vegetables, the state's second hottest agricultural product, take in a mere $5.7 billion. And California's famous grapes? A piddly $2.6 billion.

During lengthy operation in the grow room (longer than five to 10 minutes), turn the CO_2 off. There is no need for the gardener to be in an environment of elevated CO_2 levels, although 1000 ppm is harmless to humans and pets. Make sure that CO_2 is emitted only when the lights are on.

"The understanding of 'evolutionary consciousness' is perhaps the most important thing lacking in spiritual practices today. This means that there are aspects of reality that have not yet arisen in our consciousness."
~Ken Wilber

Bamboo stakes that are 2 feet tall are placed in each container. The stakes will be used in the future to help support weaker branches. The light cycle was increased to 19.5 hours and the dark cycle reduced to 4.5 hours. The diameter of several of the plants has reached the width of the containers. The light cycle will be increased incrementally until it reaches 23 or 24 hours of light before switching to flowering (12 on 12 off).

Despite 70+ years of criminal prohibition, marijuana still remains widely popular among Americans, with over 102 million (41 percent of the U.S. population) having used it during their lifetimes.

Many of the plants now have five nodes. The light cycle was increased to 20 hours; the dark cycle reduced to four hours. It is not necessary to increase the light schedule, but it is encouraged. A plant needs a minimum of 16 hours of light during the vegetative stage, but grows faster with more light.

CO₂

When you are
present in
this moment,
you break the
continuity of your
story, of past,
and future.

To match the changes in the light cycle, the CO_2 timer was adjusted accordingly to 20 hours on, and four hours off.

DAY
10

A kilogram of green leafy matter found in a 2700 year old grave in the Gobi Desert of Mongolia was identified as the world's oldest marijuana stash, say researchers. They believe the grave was of a shaman from the Gushi people.

By Day 10, the strains are showing obvious differences. Organize the containers so similar strains are grouped together. Taller, faster growing strains will block light from adjacent plants, causing stunting or death to shorter but worthy plants. Place these taller plants along the sides of the garden so they don't shadow their neighbors.

GROCK: to understand, appreciate actively and profoundly, fully comprehend; also, to think about, listen to, play, or contemplate something or someone with full love and understanding, even ecstasy. Often done stoned.

The containers were rotated 180 degrees today. This will be the last rotation because rotating the plants as the branches grow beyond the diameter of the container can lead to branch breakage. All plants should be green, healthy, and show vigorous new growth.

With 5 percent of the global population, the United States holds 25 percent of the world's prisoners. It leads in both the absolute number of prisoners—more than 2.1 million—and in per capita incarceration rates, and the numbers keep increasing as they have every year since the early 1980. *Cannabis Culture, 2008*

Each plant was given a half-gallon of water. The light cycle was increased to 23 hours and the dark cycle reduced to one hour. The light was lowered one inch.

"I gave my life to become the person I am right now. Was it worth it?"
~Richard Bach

Check the CO_2 tank level, and inspect the room for air leaks, especially at the exhaust fan and ducting connections. When tape heats and cools repeatedly it loses adhesion, making leaks more likely. The CO_2 timer was adjusted to mirror the light cycle of 23 hours on, one hour off.

DAY
13

Snoop Dogg was in four movies in 2001: *Training Day*, *The Wash*, *Bones*, and *Baby Boy*. He smokes a blunt in each of them.

Tonight the light cycle was switched to flowering: plants will receive 12 hours of uninterrupted darkness between 9 p.m. and 9 a.m. every day for the rest of their life cycle. At this point, the plants range in height from 3 to 8 inches. More important than plant height is the number of nodes. The number of nodes on a plant is a true indicator of plant maturity. These plants have an average of six primary nodes. Primary nodes are the ones that grow off the main stem.

CO₂

Presidents
George W. Bush,
Bill Clinton and
Barack Obama
all admit to
having smoked
weed.

The CO_2 timer was updated to match the new light cycle. CO_2 levels were increased today to 1300 ppm. It is easy to make adjustments to CO_2 levels using the Fuzzy Logic Controller.

"To be good just
because it has
become a habit
to be good is not
freedom either."
~Paramahansa
Yogananda

A healthy plant with vigorous new growth and at least four nodes is ready to be switched to flower-ing. Doing so with fewer than four nodes significantly reduces yield. Inducing flowering with more than 12 nodes is unlikely to increase yield unless special lighting accommodations are made. A single static light cannot penetrate the canopy of a clustered multi-plant garden; this lack of light penetration is why growing large plants indoors does not necessarily equal larger yields.

Recent interest in hemp seeds as a food source rises with the awareness of the nutritional need for omega-6 and omega-3 essential fatty acids, as well as the need for cheap sources of protein to feed a burgeoning world population. Hemp seeds fill both of these requirements.

A few small necrotic (dead tissue) areas are seen on the lower leaves on one of the plants. The rest of the plant looks fine and it has vigorous new growth. There is no concern with such small spots, but this needs to be watched. If the new growth on a plant is healthy, vigorous, and the newest leaves are larger than the previous sets of leaves, this plant can almost always be considered healthy, regardless of a few minor dead spots.

"Manifestation is showing a presence—when conditions are sufficient, something manifests itself. And that is not a beginning, that is a continuation also. It's like a beautiful cloud in the sky—that is a manifestation: Before being a cloud, the cloud has been other things like water, vapor, heat and so on."
~Thich Nhat Hanh

Giant leaves are very common on plants started from seed, compared to plants started from clones. This plant is only 16 days old and already has a leaf larger than an adult male's hand. This plant also has leaves with seven serrated fingers. As the room fills with foliage, a fan can be useful. There should always be gentle leaf movement created by circulating air.

"It is not the language but the speaker that we want to understand."
~Veda Upanishads

CO_2 is heavier than the air in the room. Use an oscillating or centrifugal fan to gently stir CO_2 from the ground of the grow room, making it accessible to all the plants.

DAY
17

Oakland, California, voters approved the nation's first cannabis business tax, Measure F, by 79.9 percent on July 22, 2009.

Growth rate is at its peak. The plants will continue at this rate of growth until the third or fourth week of flowering. During this flourishing stage, water, room temperature, and air flow should be carefully monitored. Plants in ideal grow environments, receiving everything they need, have almost unbelievable growth in this period. Leaves should be dark green: Brown tips often signal nutrient overdose.

"Self- realization
is immortality
in an entirely
new sense: not
everlasting life
but beyond death
and life alike."
~Eknath
Easwaran

Sixth day of flowering and the stems are all pure green. This is an ideal situation. The main stem on most plants is at least as thick as a pencil.

Living cannabis plants are about 80 percent water. Perfectly dried marijuana contains about 10 to 15 percent water or moisture content (MC). Material below 10 percent MC becomes too brittle and disintegrates. Fungi cannot grow below 15 percent MC.

The canopy of the garden is so dense that direct light is no longer reaching the soil. The different strains are different heights and growing at different speeds. Once a plant is shorter and receives less light than the other plants, it enters a quick downward spiral. Branches become spindly and yield is reduced 50 to 90 percent. To combat this, raise the shorter plants using wooden blocks or other supports. Raising the shorter plants prevents them from getting choked out.

Proposition 19, also known as the Regulate, Control, and Tax Cannabis Act of 2010, was on the Nov. 2, 2010, California statewide ballot as an initiated state statute. It received 4,622,626 yes votes, more than the Republican candidate for governor.

A happy odorless 80 °F garden. The plants were given 12 ounces of water each. Remember to adjust the water pH level to 6.8 to 7.0. Two of the plants are showing male traits such as greater spacing between nodes and taller height than other plants of the same strain.

CO₂

In New Mexico, one-fourth of more than 1,600 medical marijuana patients are Post-Traumatic Stress Disorder sufferers (NPR 2011).

In a CO_2-rich environment the plants flourish at slightly higher temperatures. Temperatures up to 90 °F will not harm the plants.

DAY
21

"Silence is a
source of great
strength."
~Lao Tzu

Ten male plants were removed today. Male plants have growth that look like tiny rosebuds at the base of the nodes. To prevent pollination, remove male plants before the flowers open. If already blooming (resembling pale yellow daisies), cut at the base of the main stem and carefully place in trash bags. Disturbing male flowers creates airborne pollen which can pollinate female flowers, producing seeds, and a significantly inferior quality ganja. This is *no bueno*.

The Library of Congress found that, "While the hemp paper in volumes 300 to 400 years old is still strong, 97 percent of the books, printed between 1900 and 1937 on tree paper, will be useable for less than 50 years." Hemp paper can be recycled seven to eight times, compared with only three times for wood pulp paper.

Spread out the remaining plants to occupy the entire grow space. The remaining plants were watered with a half-gallon of pH 6.5 water. Foliage is dense, lush, and green.

Absolute stillness is the field of all possibilities; it is beyond time and space. It is the unmoving center of all action. It is the quiet place from which all vibration originates. It is a method of connecting with divinity. It is the source of all manifestation.

Extra attention is required to identify suspected male plants. Male plants usually show their sex before female plants. Male flowers show first on primary nodes on the main stem.

There are several other non-wood paper sources. Ed Rosenthal's book, *Hemp Today* (1994), ranked potential paper species in order of importance: sugarcane, bamboo, straws, kenaf, mesta, hemp, abaca, sisal, henequen, jute, ramie, flax, and sunhemp. Hemp is ranked first for plants that will grow well all over American temperate climates.

Another male was found today. This is a bit disconcerting and causes angst. More males (see circle) are being found than expected. The goal is to harvest a pound. If more plants need to be removed, there may not be enough to get the desired yield of a pound.

"I don't say
I'm enlightened
and you're
endarkened.
I do not say that.
I don't feel myself
to be enlightened
in a world of
endarkened
people."
~Douglas Harding

The first female plant reveals a white hair! You can see the white hair, the female stigma (center of this picture), coming from a node. It took 11 days into the flowering cycle to identify the first female plant. Only female plants produce sensimilla—seedless marijuana, or female buds that have not been fertilized by male plants.

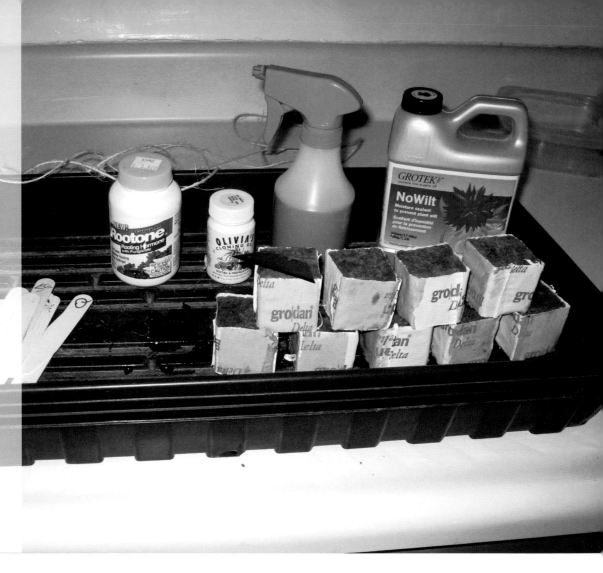

No one has ever died from marijuana overdose. Tests on mice have shown that the levels of cannabinoids required for overdose opposed to levels resulting in a high is a ratio is 40,000:1. The ratio for alcohol? Generally 4:1 to 10:1.

Cuttings or clones can be trimmed from your existing plant and nurtured until they sprout roots and become plants of their own. Clones have the exact genetic qualities as their parent. A female plant ensures that the clones will be female. Gather the cloning tools: razor blades, cloning gel, rooting hormone, markers, cloning trays, and covers.

Successful cloning can be achieved by following simple steps: First, soak rockwool cubes in water set to a pH of 5.0. The cubes should soak completely submerged for at least 15 minutes. Note: Cloning is not necessary; moreover, your plants may not be big enough at this time to clone.

Find a healthy plant, and trim a branch that has at least three nodes on it. Using clones shortens growing time because the seedling stage is skipped. Find the spot on the cutting that is half-inch below the third node from the top. Make a diagonal, clean cut with a sharp and clean razor blade (A). Make another cut, removing the first node from the bottom of the cutting (B).

You should now be holding a cutting that resembles figure C. It is also okay to make smaller or larger clones, with more or less nodes. The cutting should be green and not woody.

Dip the cutting into root powder or root gel (D). The cloning solution should cover the clones first node (which has been cut clean of foliage). Gently insert the cutting into a hole at the top of the cube. The hole should be snug, yet big enough to accommodate the cutting without causing the branch to bend (E).

Hang a 20-watt compact fluorescent bulb six to 14 inches from the tray of clones (F). The clones should be kept between 70 to 80 °F. Keep cubes moist. Fill trays with pH 5.0 water, rather than water from the tap. Clones need a minimum of 16 hours of light. Don't let light from your cloning area leak into your flowering grow room.

Be meticulous about marking clones accurately so that you know the parents of each clone. Without clear identification, you can't make informed decisions. For example, if you have limited height in your garden, you may want to keep clones from the shortest plants. It's fine to take clones up to 4 to 6 weeks into flowering; they will just take 2 to 4 weeks longer to root.

"To err is
human;
to forgive,
divine."
~Alexander
Pope

The light was raised 2 inches today, because some of the foliage was touching the glass hood. If the hood/reflector was not air cooled, the plants would have suffered severe burning as they grew close to the reflector.

Almost 48 percent of all drug arrests nationwide are for marijuana. In 2007 alone, more than 775,000 Americans entered the criminal justice system after an arrest for marijuana possession.

A couple of the largest leaves in the garden are curling and new growth looks fabulous. This curling is caused by the plant transferring nitrogen from the lower leaves—which are deprived of light—to the new growth. The canopy is so dense that this lack of light would occur even if these plants were outdoors in sunlight.

"We cannot change anything until we accept it. Condemnation does not liberate, it oppresses."
~Carl Jung

The plants are thriving. Currently this grow has a CO_2 level of 1300 ppm.

In 1906 Congress passed the Pure Food and Drug Act, which required the labeling of cannabis and the amount contained in over-the-counter remedies and food.

The tallest plants are 1 inch from the reflector hood. Vertical growth usually stops around three weeks after the 12 hours light/12 hours dark flowering regime is induced. These plants have been growing an inch taller every day for the past 10 days.

"Give up defining yourself to yourself or to others. You won't die. You will come to life. And don't be concerned with how others define you. When they define you, they are limiting themselves, so it's their problem. You can only lose something that you have, but you cannot lose something that you are."
~Eckhart Tolle

This is a typical look for a flowering female plant that is beginning to swell. The tips of the branches look like a collision of foliage.

"At present, I am mainly observing the physical motion of mountains, water, trees, and flowers. One is everywhere reminded of similar movements in the human body, of similar impulses of joy and suffering in plants."
~Egon Schiele

White stigmas are abundant and obvious to even the layman's eye. The odor from the garden has increased significantly.

CO₂

"Legalizing
marijuana will
break the back
of cannabis
crime-syndicate
and local
communities
will reap the
benefits."
~Judge Arnold
Gravinski

The 20-pound CO_2 tank was found empty today and was replaced. The valve must be closed, and the regulator unscrewed. The first tank lasted a month. The room was checked for leaks and loose connections. None were found.

"Legalization of drugs would end the drug war and related violence in Mexico."
~Bryan Gonzales, U.S. Border Patrol agent

The growth is explosive, branches and stems are green. A healthy plant is easily recognized.

"A garden requires patient labor and attention. Plants do not grow merely to satisfy ambitions or to fulfill good intentions. They thrive because someone expended effort on them."
~Liberty Hyde Bailey

One plant is getting too close to the light, so one of its branches is "pinched," letting it lean gently to the side away from the light. To pinch, find a spot about two-thirds up a branch (either from the soil or nearest node); gently squeeze and release with firm pressure until it leans over. Some growers roll the branch between the fingers while applying firm pressure. The branch may need to lean against another branch or be tied to a stick until the pinched spot hardens—24 to 48 hours.

Walmart fired Joseph Casias of Battle Creek, Michigan, for marijuana use. Casias is a cancer patient who uses medical marijuana at his oncologist's recommendation.

Plant foliage is touching the glass on the reflector. This has been going on for two days and the leaves appear fine. Three factors are allowing this to occur without burning: The lack of heat emitted by the air-cooled lamp, the light mover, and the exhaust fan are keeping temperature levels low enough so leaves don't burn. An oscillating fan blowing air around the room is another helpful addition.

"If the love within your mind is lost and you see other beings as enemies, then no matter how much knowledge or education or material comfort you have, only suffering and confusion will ensue."
~Dalai Lama

Explosive, vigorous growth is occurring at every node. This growth during flowering will translate into heavier yields! The plants that were on wooden blocks (risers) are now touching the light and the blocks were removed to lower them.

DAY 36

In 1937 Congress passes the Marijuana Tax Act in response to growing fear around the drug. It effectively outlawed marijuana. Only those who pay an excise tax for certain authorized uses are allowed to possess it.

Each plant was watered with 1 gallon of water. It is becoming clear which plants will have larger buds. The spacing between nodes is usually the give-away. This plant has a lot of space between nodes and this characteristic is not ideal when going for a big yield. It is important to keep a good record of plant genetics, so that you don't continue to grow plants that don't suit your needs. The general rule of thumb is, shorter node spacing equals greater yield.

"The beauty of a
lake reflects the
beauty around it.
When the mind is
still, the beauty
of the Self is seen
reflected in it."
~BKS Iyengar

Four plants are bent over using string, and one is pinched. You can see in the photo the plant juice oozing from the stalk where the plant was pinched. The light is also raised an inch. The catch trays that were full after yesterday's watering are now empty. The plants are drinking a lot of water, helping to fuel their mega-growth. The clones are examined but no roots are visible.

Mariuana is a plant that can and has been used for a multitude of purposes since at least 8000 B.C.E.

A couple of the leaves had burn marks so the lights were raised another inch. You want the light as near to the foliage as possible without burning the buds. This is a fine balancing act. A burned leaf or two (or six) is okay. A burned bud or cola is NOT okay! The buds are starting to swell and becoming recognizable as magazine-quality centerfold material!

"A morning-glory at my window satisfies me more than the metaphysics of books."
~Walt Whitman

One of the plants appears droopy, and is given half-gallon of pH adjusted water. You don't want plants on individual watering cycles as it is much easier to tend to a garden when all the plants are on the same watering regimen. However, with four different strains you have to accommodate the needs of the individual plants. Roots can be seen at the bottom of the containers. This is NOT a sign that the plants need to be transplanted.

"The prestige of government has undoubtedly been lowered considerably by the prohibition law. For nothing is more destructive of respect for the government and the law of the land than passing laws which cannot be enforced. It is an open secret that the dangerous increase of crime in this country is closely connected with this."
~Albert Einstein

The light was raised another inch today. Better safe than sorry! Vertical growth should be finished and raising the light from here on out should not be needed. Two more plants receive a half-gallon of water today. Swelling buds, clusters of hairs, and the aroma of high-grade ganja is abundant.

CO₂

"There is only
one person that
will be with you
your entire life.
The only sane
choice is to love
this person."
~SeeMoreBuds

The buds seem to be developing faster than normal. I suspect this is a reaction to the supplement-ed CO_2. When the tank has CO_2, the release valve makes a gentle clicking sound when it turns on and off. You may hear this several hundred times in a 12-hour cycle. If you don't hear this sound, check the tank level—it may be empty.

Cannabis was outlawed in California in 1913.

Lower leaves are starting to fall. It is a good idea to remove dead (pure yellow or brown) leaves from the grow room, including leaves still attached to the plant. Dead leaves normally detach from the plant with a gentle touch. Dead leaves attract bugs and worse—molds.

DAY
42

Always focus only
on the wellbeing
of all others.

A single plant was watered today. The plants were thoroughly examined one by one. It is good to take notes of any burns, dead leaves, broken branches, signs of pests, and areas of the garden that are not receiving adequate light. Attentiveness to garden details prevents unwanted surprises.

Making up your
own answer
is easier than
making space for
the truth.

Today is the first day crystals were seen on the plants. The odor is skunky and potent. After notic-
ing dry soil and a lack in vibrancy, the plants were each given a half-gallon of water.

Cannabis
is the third
most popular
recreational drug
after alcohol and
tobacco.

Six yellow leaves were pulled, and two plants were given a half-gallon of water. A couple more burned leaves were noticed, but the burns were minor. All the plants are around 26 inches tall. Most of the plants have been pinched or tied down. The plants are actually still growing vertically, but only about an eighth-inch per day. The density of the foliage prevents perfect light distribution, yet the garden sure looks beautiful.

Man finds salvation not in thinking about himself but in working for others.

Among the top of a grower's "joyful moments" is the first root sightings on clones. There is always excitement when the magic of cloning shows its success in the form of young, vibrant, succulent, white roots. The clone looks a little sad, but take a look at the roots—this baby is perfect! Healthy new root growth is the foundation of success. The 2-inch cubes are transferred to 4-inch cubes. The 4-inch cubes are first prepared as described on page 10.

"Subjecting cannabis to a licensed, regulated system would generate hundreds of millions of dollars for health care at a time when Washington's budget is being decimated."
~ Dr. William Robertson

The light was raised today another 2 inches.

In 1930 the U.S. Treasury Department created the Federal Bureau of Narcotics.

Not as much CO_2 is being used each day because lights are off half the time, and less gas is being emitted.

"He plants trees
to benefit another
generation."
~Caecilius
Statius

Everything looks marvelous. Crystal formation is abundant. The odor is still manageable, but any disturbance of the plants spikes the odor significantly (like pinching a small nug found in a bag of chronic, but 1000-fold). The leaves are a solid and even green, not blotchy. A couple more small (size of a nickle) burns are spotted. These burns are a small price to pay for the benefits achieved from having the light as close as possible to the foliage.

The plants are drinking a lot of water now. The room feels more humid as watering and transpiration increases. Two of the plants are each given 1 gallon of water. The crystals are forming on top of each other. The clones have roots showing out the bottom of the 4-inch rockwool and are ready for planting into a permanent medium.

"Breath is the bridge which connects life to consciousness, which unites your body to your thought."
~Thich Nhat Hanh

This is a typical and picture-perfect leaf after several weeks of flowering. In the flowering process, the leaves lose their green pigment and turn pale yellow. At this point they can and should be removed. Fewer leaves in the garden allows for greater light penetration, better air flow, and reduces the possibility of mold and fungus.

Researchers from Canada and the former Soviet Union found that wheat will grow faster when exposed to special ultrasonic and musical sounds.

Temperatures in the room today reached 90-plus °F. The plants were checked every couple hours. The plant leaves were pointed more vertical than normal, which is one way the plants cope with extreme heat. The door of the garden was left open almost the entire day to help air flow and manage heat.

CO₂

"We think that
the point is to
pass the test
or to overcome
the problem,
but the truth is
that things don't
really get solved.
They come
together and they
fall apart."
~Pema Chodron

The door to the grow room was accidently left ajar a half-inch for several hours today. This probably caused an excess of CO_2 to be released from the tank. Close attention will be given to the tank to make sure it is replaced as soon as it is empty. Leaving the door open during the night cycle and allowing a significant light leak would have been a more serious oversight.

DAY
51

"THC is the engine of cannabis, and the terpenes are the steering wheel."
~Ed Rosenthal

All of the plants received 1 gallon of water today. An hour after the plants were watered the humidity increased significantly. More than 100 dead leaves were collected from the grow room and disposed. The temperatures in the grow room surpassed 90 °F again. The temperature in the grow room was high because outside temperatures were over 100 °F.

"Only by allowing every movement of thought, stillness comes into being."
~Krishnamurti

The swelling buds on the nodes are starting to collide into each other, creating beautiful colas.

The IRS ruled (2011) that dispensaries cannot deduct standard business expenses such as payroll, security or rent. The is based on an obscure portion of the tax code passed in 1982, at the height of Reagan administration's War on Drugs. The law, originally targeted at drug kingpins and cartels, bans tax deductions related to "trafficking in controlled substances."

The top colas look delicious and are tempting to sample. Three plants received 1 gallon of water each.

CO$_2$

See possessions
as things to use
when you need
them, and not
as a definition of
who you are.

With CO$_2$ supplementation, the plants can withstand 90 °F temperatures; some strains will even thrive in these conditions. Good air flow on such hot days is vital. If the door must be left open on a garden supplemented with CO$_2$ in order to regulate heat, the tank should be turned off. Turn it back on when the room is again sealed.

Cannabis was first recognized as medically beneficial 5000 years ago in the reign of the Chinese emperor Shen Nung. It was used to treat malaria, constipation, and even absent-mindedness.

Stunning colas are on every plant now. Look closely every day for bugs, mold, and fungus. This is cheap insurance—hot temperatures and dense buds are a perfect storm for mold!

"There is one way
of breathing that
is shameful and
constricted. Then
there's another
way: a breath of
love that takes
you all the way to
infinity." ~Rumi

The main stems of every plant have colas at least 4 inches long. These swollen colas conceal the stem and possess a density that is a trademark of growing with 1000-watt HPS bulbs. Gardening exclusively with compact fluorescent lights can yield dense buds but it is usually just the main stem cola. These plants have colas on secondary growth that are as big and dense as the main stem cola. 1000 watts of HPS light offers deep penetration and consistency throughout the garden.

In 2011 over 50,000 people were arrested for marijuana possession "open to public view," a 69 percent jump from 2005.

All of the plants received 1 gallon of pH-adjusted water.

CO_2

How can there be peace when we are fighting?

The CO_2 tank is replaced today. The depleted 20-pound tank is swapped for a full tank at a local hydroponics store.

DAY
57

U.S. Border
Patrol doubled
the number of
agents from
10,000 in 2004 to
21,000 in 2011.

Outstanding growth continues. Occasional brown hairs appear throughout the garden. Many old school growers consider a plant ready to harvest when it displays 70 to 80 percent brown hairs.

DAY

58

Arrests for drug
law violations
in 2012 are
expected to
exceed the
1.6 million
arrests. About
900,000 of the
arrests will be
for cannabis
possession.
One out of 180
Americans will
be arrested
in 2012 on
drug-related
violations.

High temperatures combined with the plants' increasing water consumption and transpiration is a good recipe for dreaded bud rot. Circulating air helps combat this.

CO₂

During his campaign for the 2008 U.S. Presidential election, President Barack Obama had a decidedly different answer than Bill Clinton on whether he ever smoked marijuana. "When I was a kid I inhaled frequently," said Obama. "That was the point."

The CO₂ tubes were adjusted today so they did not touch any of the sticky buds.

"The intellect is not the best tool for solving life's great questions. Rather, it is a survival tool better suited for procuring your daily bread and butter."
~ Tommy Hellsten

Fungus! A small infestation is spotted on this drooping branch. The bud is gently wrapped in a plastic bag and snipped off with sharp scissors. You do not want any fungus dust to spread. All of the colas will now be examined daily. I have Ed Rosenthal's Zero Tolerance Fungicide ready to spray, in case powdery mildew breaks out.

DAY
60

Everybody who buys a gun must fill out ATF Form 4473, which asks: "Are you an unlawful user of, or addicted to, marijuana or any depressant, stimulant, narcotic drug, or any other controlled substance?" Answer yes, and you don't get the gun. Falsely answer no, and you've just committed a crime.

All the plants received 1 gallon of pH-adjusted water today. The closet door was left open to keep the grow room temperature below 85 °F.

"Wisdom is
tricky.
One can
understand
the world, and
nothing at all."
- R. Douglas

No more mold has been spotted. A magnifying glass is used daily for examinations. It is usually a dead serrated single-blade leaf protruding from a cola that reveals mold inside.

In 2011, federal regulators cracked down on banks in Colorado, California, and Michigan that had previously conducted business with medical cannabis dispensaries, forbidding these financial institutions from allowing cash deposits or processing credit or debit cards from state or locally approved canna-businesses.

Plants received 1 gallon of pH-adjusted water today.

See possessions
as things to use
when you need
them, and not
as a definition of
who you are.

The oscillating fan has been on at night without the carbon scrubber. Big mistake. The fan was disturbing the plants and causing the immediate vicinity around the apartment complex to reek of skunk. One of the neighbors mentioned a "skunk" smell. Lesson learned. The plants will reek constantly when they are being blown around by a fan and this odor can easily be managed by leaving the carbon filter on continuously.

CO_2 levels continue to be maintained at 1300 ppm. The CO_2 supplemented garden seems to be a week ahead of schedule. Plant development is obviously thicker than in the non-CO_2 grow.

"Non-human
animals don't
measure
anything that
they do...yet they
still do what they
do...and they are
pretty amazing."
~Hayley Parlen

Plants received another gallon of pH-adjusted water.

DAY
65

For most of human history, marijuana has been completely legal. It is not a recently discovered plant. Marijuana has been illegal for less than 1 percent of the time that it's been in use. Its known uses go back further than 7000 B.C. and it was legal as recently as when Ronald Reagan was a boy.

A forest has taken over the closet. The excitement of a harvest looms!

If we follow our
unique interests
over a lifetime,
we will find there
is a continuous
growth in our
understanding
and appreciation
of what we have
experienced.
Most importantly,
we will feel we
had led a full and
meaningful life.

All of the plants were removed from the closet to thoroughly search for mold/fungus growth. The process is tedious and slow as the many heavy branches with dense buds must be treated gently. It is easy to snap and lose branches as harvest time approaches. The plants need more time in the flowering cycle, but they are far enough along that if bud rot is spotted an immediate and complete harvest may have to be considered. No mold was found.

Five to 10 percent of the crystals are turning an amber color. All of the clones are rooted and are ready to go in the grow room.

By trusting in the unknowable force of stillness, you will find that your gifts and your true passions will flow through you with ease. You will begin to know who you truly are. And you will begin to create the world that you truly believe in. Stillness is absolute.

Every cola is magazine-centerfold material.

Harvest time is near and some difficult decisions need to be made. Now is the time to inspect your plants and make critical observations that will allow you to chose which strain(s) to keep for the next grow. Traits of the top performers based on your select criteria (weight, odor, smoke, growth, height, etc.) will continue in future grows. The other clones will be given away or disposed of.

You can wake up
and at the same
moment you
will realize that
you have been
asleep.

The buds are large, swollen, and causing all the branches to lean. The plants are sticky and stinky.
Working with or touching the plants in any way requires serious cleaning before going out in the
public. The odor is no joke and should not be taken lightly.

Today the CO_2 is turned off. No plants received any water in the last six days of the grow.

A close look through a magnifying glass shows the trichomes shining like crystals; the glands stand erect and are filled with resin that is turning from clear to amber or milky white. It's time to harvest.

Harvesting cannabis is a time-consuming task and any chronic you plan on selling to medical marijuana dispensaries will require meticulous manicuring. A single plant with 40 grams of chronic can take as long as three hours to trim. Needle-nose type scissors work best. This type of scissors will allow trimming leaf stems close to the stalk, providing aesthetically pleasing nugs.

A simple harvest and drying method involves these steps: 1) Cut the plant from the base of the stalk; 2) Cut the plant into several manageable branches (usually five to 10 pieces for 3-feet tall indoor plants); 3) Trim each portion (branch) until only fine smoking chronic remains; 4) Hang the branch on a clothes hanger in a dark closet, or place the branch on a screen (drying rack).

Keep the drying branches in a dark room that has a gentle breeze or some air movement.

Just before the plants are fully dry (usually five to nine days), trim buds off branches and put them in glass jars or plastic bags. Seal the containers shut for 24 hours and then re-open for 12 to 24 hours, allowing the plants to breathe and release built-up moisture. Repeat this opening and closing every 12 to 24 hours a couple times, or until the plants have less than 10 percent of their moisture. This curing process is vital to preserving your chronic and avoiding mold growth.

Four TGA strains were grown in this book: Jack the Ripper, Space Queen, Querkle, and Pandora's Box. These are quality strains. The first garden without CO_2 supplementation started with six seeds of each strain, for a total of 24 plants.

Here is the break down: The Jack and Querkle strains were the obvious heavyweights in this garden. For this reason the next CO_2-enhanced crop consisted of eight cloned female Jacks and eight cloned female Querkles, and the yield was nearly 2 pounds. The garden yielded 1.94 pounds (869 grams).

A garden with a good female strain, good lighting, good air flow, good growing medium, and a good gardener should harvest a pound. A small garden that grows more than a pound is often called "a golden garden." The previous pages displayed such a garden.

The CO_2 grow yielded 1.94 pounds (839 grams), which was almost twice as much as the yield from the non-CO_2 garden. This higher yield was due to two factors: First, I used only Jack the Ripper and Querkle, strains that produce more bud. Second, the use of CO_2 greatly increased my total harvest. In the CO_2 grow, the yield from the Jack and Querkle strains went from an average 39 grams per plant to an average 54 grams per plant, nearly a 40 percent increase! Based on these results, I strongly advise any grower who can afford the additional investment to use CO_2—it's well worth the extra money.

NON-CO_2 GROW			CO2 GROW	
Strain	Number of Plants	Yield/Plant Average	Number of Plants	Yield/Plant Average
JACK THE RIPPER	8	39 grams	8	54 grams
QUERKLE	8	39 grams	8	54 grams
PANDORA'S BOX	2	20 grams	N/A	
SPACE QUEEN	4	8 grams	N/A	

Glossary

Alternating nodes: When leaves grow at different heights on the axis, not directly opposite each other but in succession, alternating sides.

Clone: A genetically identical copy.

Cloning: Taking cuttings from a mother plant and making clones.

Cola: Multiple buds growing together on a single branch.

Flowering stage: This is the last stage of a plant. It produces seeds and fruit in this stage. Changing of seasons, shorter days, and shorter light periods trigger flowering. It is critical that a plant gets at least 12 hours of uninterrupted darkness every 24 hours to induce flowering.

Mother plant: A plant that is kept in a vegetative stage and used for cloning.

Necrotic: Discolored, dead tissue on a leaf.

Nodes: The point on a stem where a leaf is attached or has been attached.

Pistils: The female organs of a flower.

Ppm: Parts per million: here, the ratio of the amount of CO_2 in the air.

Secondary growth: The branch growing off of a branch that comes from the main stalk.

Sinsemilla: Flowering tops which are free of seeds from being grown in a pollen-free environment.

Stretch: The growth of spacing between nodes. Usually stretching is exaggerated when there is a shortage of light.

Trichomes: Glands growing off of the leaves and buds that contain THC.

Vegetative stage: This is the primary growth stage of a plant. The plant needs to be under 18 to 24 hours of light to stay in this stage.

Metric Conversion Chart

METRIC CONVERSION CHART

Mass

1 gram = 0.035 ounces (1/28 ounce)

1 ounce = 28.35 grams

1 pound = 16 ounces

1 kilogram = 2.2 pounds

1 pound = 0.45 kilograms

Length

1 foot = 30.5 centimeters (1/3 meter)

1 meter =3.28 feet

1 meter = 100 centimeters

1 inch = 2.54 centimeters

Area

1 square meter = 10.76 square feet

1 square foot = .09 square meters

Yield

1 ounce per square foot = 305 g per square meter

100 grams per square meter = 0.33 oz. per square foot

Temperature

15 °C = 59 °F

20 °C = 68 °F

25 °C = 72 °F

28 °C = 82 °F

30 °C = 86 °F

32 °C = 89.5 °F

35 °C = 95 ° F

To figure:

Celsius = (F - 32) x 5/9

Fahrenheit = C x 9/5 + 32

pH Adjustment

Making pH balanced water is easy, and essential for a successful grow. Add pH test solution to a water sample. Compare the color of the treated water to the chart on the back of the pH tester vial. If pH needs to be lowered, add a small amount of pH Down. If pH needs to be raised, add pH Up. Repeat this process until you get the desired pH.

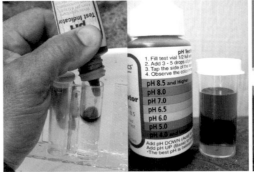

FYI - FURTHER REFERENCE

THE NEXT STEP...

Congratulations! You now know how to grow your first pound. What's the next step? Bigger and better!

Let's Grow a Pound has provided the foundation you will need to complete your first crop and an introduction to growing that will catapult you forward. As an individual, the art & science of growing is something that you will continue to refine with future crops, better tools, developed techniques, and alternative growing methods. As you expand the size of your garden, you'll find that there are many options when it comes to lights anad nutrients.

Check out some of these items that will be sure to take you to the next level of growing — from a closet to a room!

QUANTUM BALLASTS
AND QUANTUM MASSIVE HOODS

Bigger and better lighting = bigger and better buds! Quality lighting contributes directly to yield. When it comes to big yields, lighting is the number one element. Quantum ballasts are generally considered the "cream of the crop" when it comes to digital ballasts. Keeping a larger room with multiple lights cool is important for your next-level grow. Quantum digital ballasts also feature dimming options that allow you to lower output level to avoid frying your clones and seedlings.

When you move up to a larger room with more lights, you need to keep things chill with proper ventilation, ducting and a well designed, tightly sealed reflector hood. Quantum Massive lighting reflectors have one of the largest lighting footprints in the hydroponics industry, delivering more premium lumens to a wider area in your garden than any standard reflector. Its highly reflective surface also ensures that almost no lumens are wasted from bulb to plants.

Available from C.A.P. —www.capcontrollers.com—and hydroponic stores everywhere

RASTA BOB'S

Rasta Bob's is a great line of effective garden products Here's a quick rundown:

Death Mite Spray: Spider mites can ruin a great crop. This all-natural formula will banish them from your garden without using chemicals that can hurt you.

One Love Bloom Enhancer: Pack those extra grams onto each bud and enhance resin /oil production, as well as delicious aromas!

Rasta Roots: Experienced growers truly know their plant root zone. Mix this with your soil or add it to your hydroponic reservoir to deliver a root zone inoculation of beneficial microbes for efficient nutrient absorption!

Humic Acid: Humic Acid frees up beneficial nutrients in soil, provides a carbon food source for beneficial microbes and aids in the absorption of micronutrients.

Fulvic Acid: Fulvic acids increase resistance to pathogens and disease and enhance nutrient uptake.

Blackstrap Molasses: A quick and easy source of energy for microbes and beneficials in plant root zones, as well as a strong carbohydrate boost.

Available from C.A.P. —www.capcontrollers.com—and hydroponic stores everywhere

PURE ESSENTIALS BLACK LABEL NUTRIENTS

You've finally made it through a couple of grows and are getting your skills dialed in. Learn to introduce the minimum nutrients needed for maximum growing results.

VEG: Two-part vegetative nutrient delivers incredibly fast growth and superior structural integrity.

BUD: This professionally blended two-part formula is made of purest raw ingredients to max growth during the flowering stage.

ROOT ENHANCE: Stimulate root growth to EXPLOSIVE levels with this breakthrough product, increasing vegetative growth and harvests.

BUD ENHANCE: Help your plants express their genetics to their fullest! An organic-base stimulates enzymatic processes and lets plants focus on the creation of dense flower sets.

FLUSH: Correct over-feeding and salt build-up, leaving your harvest tasting sweeter than ever.

ZYM: More than ten types of enzymes, with vitamins and exotic plant extracts, accelerate cycling of decaying root matter and discourage colonies of harmful pathogenic organisms.

SeeMoreBuds
on DVD!

"This dude is like the Martha Stewart of weed growing"
~ *Vapor Magazine*

"SeeMoreBuds—I love this guy"
~ *Ed Rosenthal*

Free Previews: www.SeeMoreBuds.com

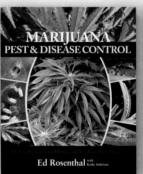
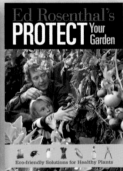